Before the Distance

Virus Poems
by
Pasquale Trozzolo

A Publication of The Poetry Box®

Poems ©2020 Pasquale Trozzolo
All rights reserved.

Editing & Book Design: Shawn Aveningo Sanders
Cover Art: Dan Vanderhoof (danvanderhoof.com)
Cover Design: Shawn Aveningo Sanders
Author Photo: Paul Versluis (paulversluis.com)

No part of this book may be reproduced in any manner whatsoever without permission from the author, except in the case of brief quotations embodied in critical essays, reviews and articles.

ISBN: 978-1-948461-74-0
Library of Congress Control Number: 2020913548
Printed in the United States of America.
Wholesale Distribution via Ingram.

Published by The Poetry Box®, 2020
Portland, Oregon
ThePoetryBox.com

*To my granddaughter Sophia Rose
and all the members of the class of 2020
for your losses and your gains.*

– Contents –

Graduation	9
Reputation	11
Heavy	13
Blue	15
Contender	17
About Why	19
Cope-Outs	21
Do You	23
Missing	25
Slip	27
Before the Distance	29
Opening Games	31
Synchronized	33
Twister	35
It Is	37
Restaurant	39
Backyard	41
Miss Remembering	43
Walls	45
On Sale	47
Q the Day	49
Acknowledgments	51
Praise for *Before the Distance*	53
About the Author	55
About The Poetry Box®	56

*I never hear the word
"Escape"
Without a quicker blood,
A sudden expectation,
A flying attitude.*

~Emily Dickinson

Graduation is a milestone we share with friends and family. An official declaration of completion. Success. A gateway. A right somehow lost to the class of 2020. A loss that will bind them like no other—perhaps for good.

Graduation
~for Sophia

Although she did not ask
Questions hang in the air
Like fog clouding what comes next
Waiting patiently to consume
Nothing is clear—only mist.

Will we see gowns?
Will caps fly?
Will we remain suspended,
Unable to escape,
A distant stage our only set?

Although she did not ask,
Questions remain.
Where are my flowers?
Will there be music?
When is my party?

I emailed one of my long-lost cousins last night after a day filled with making contact with others both near and far. Like some sort of nice guy, I'm sending happy messages and such. What's up with that? This social distancing stuff is drawing me in—deeper.

Reputation

I haven't been this nice to people since, ever.
Admittedly
I'm mostly calling, texting, tagging, emailing
People I like
Mostly.
And Facebook, come on
Do I really "like" it or
Just being nice?
If this virus doesn't kill me
It's going to ruin my
Respectability.

This really is thin. I almost missed it. Everything seems so big and hard and dangerous that we often forget the scale—the one that measures us like a pebble of sand. So, if you're feeling it, why not write a poem? Even a thin one might make someone smile.

Heavy

This
Is
A
Thin
Poem.

It's
Okay
To
Like
It.

You
Might
Lose
Weight.

Painting seems like so much fun—to be able to cover canvas and uncover so much. Oh, to be stuck at home painting! While I can't paint, I have learned to be a good admirer, especially of abstract expressionists— that would be me, if only, like Helen Frankenthaler in a field of color. But no—I'm left to words and I stand behind these words, pretending not to care—like an abstract expressionist.

Blue

If I could paint,
The picture would appear.
In colors of abstraction
I'd hide my many fears.

Maybe you would see them.
Some of you might not.
It's not my care
There's no paint there.
The pen is all I got.

You cannot see it from up close
Like pointillism dots.
No hook, no frame,
Or special name.
Paper's all I've got.

Behind this art
A story lies
Well hidden by the hue.
It's yours to find,
But keep in mind
There may be too
Much blue.

Sheltering in place won't protect us from reflecting. I'm usually optimistic about my past. I like my history— mostly. But even with little regret I wonder what could have been. If only. Did I miss a friendship? Was there a love that could have been? My list of what's done is longer than what's left undone and for that I am grateful. Still I wonder what was left unnoticed, unexplored. Could I have been a better...?

Contender

Whose smile did I ignore?
What cry did I not hear?
Whose hand did I not take?
What kiss did never tell?
What love did we not make?
How much is never known?
What love we let escape?
What new could have been?
What wonder could have flowed?

For most of my life why has been the guiding question —as in question just about everything. I'll admit that I got very good at questioning and preached a fair bit about finding your why, the search as old as the ages. Today I woke up in a when frame of mind. As in when will this be over? not why did it happen?

About Why

I don't like why
It's so demanding
And discouraging
Why should why matter so much
When is so much better.

Why is the question
When is the answer.

Like when we kiss
Not why we might
Like when we are born
Not why we die
Like when we write
Not why we try.

How are your coping skills—anything to share? No judgment.

Cope-Outs

Yes, that's me
And I'm not alone.
We're everywhere.
Facebook, Insta, the Tube and Twit
Everywhere.
Teaching, singing, dancing, painting.
Some of us share bad poems.
Brave cope-outs
That's who we are.
If you haven't tried it
Go ahead. Cope out!
You'll feel better.
Guaranteed.

This gloomy morning I got lost in a stream of thought of days and people past. With luck, you have a long list of friends and a lifetime of shared experiences. Along the way, you may have encountered a precious few who came into your life for just a moment or two but somehow made a lasting impression. While they may not be on your list of current friends, they are with you still.

Do You

Remember me?
Forgotten
Yet there
Cemented in your past.
Are you alive?
And well?
Do you remember that song?
Our song?
Precious and Few
I remember you
And our moments
Quiet and blue like the sky.
Did you find love?
Did you find your way home?
Do you remember?

Loss, especially abrupt loss, needs no color. No explanation. No rescue. Loss is just loss—and hurt. And no matter our station, we all lose sooner or later. Here's hoping it's later, much later.

Missing

Is that her
Fragrance
In the air.

Is that her
Dress
And her hair.

Is that her
Breath
On my face.

Is that her
Glance
And her lace.

Is that her
Whisper
Telling truth.

Is that her
Touch
Feeling blue.

Is that her
Heart
Still beating.

COVID feels like it falls from the sky, unrelenting, creating a storm of danger.

Slip

Sleet falls
Driven to assault me
Expert precision astounds.
Piles my path with
Slip
Pelts me in a
Storm of dangerous
Possibilities.

I'm right to be afraid.

Where is my snow?
Soft and free
Beauty in each flake.
Come snow
Take my sleet away.
Stop this freezing arrest.
Where is my snow
Pure fluff
Where?

The sun was out this afternoon and there was definitely spring and a touch of hope in the air. And yet I miss winter. What about you?

Before the Distance

Where did you go?
It was winter
Before the distance.
Why is a lonely spring already here?
Some may not miss you
But me—I do.
Winter's end is
My favorite time.
Like a lost lover
Resisting
Warming and
Cool again.
Unpredictable
Full of surprise.
False starts and wild blooms
All knuckleballs and chances.
I want winter again!
Before the distance
With a true winter's end
Without the distance.
Just the wonder and glory of a
Good-natured fight.
Where did you go winter?
Where?

Almost like the stock market our emotions rise and fall based on the news. Fake or not is ours to decide.

Opening Games

In my mind I still have places to go
People to meet, hands to hold, vacations.
Promise of normal chaos tempts me so
With reasons to believe lonely passes,
Melts this trance that infects virulently.
Are these facts to trust or just too deep in
Wine that brings hope. Are these footsteps for me
To follow or fear? Are we now coming
Back to life or is this our true decline?

I miss synchronizing. These days I stare into nothing and pass it off as work. And so, sitting in a chair, staring outside and missing my friends, I noticed dust particles in sunbeams. And since this was work after all, I needed to make something of it. So, I ask, does dust make choices?

Synchronized

Sunlight shined through the
Leaded window,
Dust particles floating through it.

Frozen in sunlight,
They continued
Turning,
Dancing,
Synchronized.

They disappeared.

Does dust make choices?
To turn,
To dance,
To synchronize?

Is their journey through
Sunlight made more
Meaningful by the company
They keep?

Mine is.

Twister, "The game that ties you up in knots," came out the year of my 8th grade and made for entertaining times at our grade school graduation parties. Little did we know as 14-year-olds that being tied up in knots stays with you long after the game is over. Anyone who has put on some years can tell you that the best moments often grow from those knots, and we are strengthened by the play. It is the twists and turns in life, just like the game, that adds the interest.

Twister

Twists
Turns
Obstacles
Challenges
Each brings its owns play
Fear or pleasure is ours to decide.
Wisely.

Looking in the mirror this morning I tried talking myself out of writing another poem but I'm so vain. I know it's true. Not Trump level but still—a bit much. And I'm not the only one. So if you can hear the music, maybe ...

It Is

You
Probably think
This poem
Is about you.
Yes, you.

Always the center of attention.
My attention.
Do you ever think
To just keep it to yourself?

You don't always need
To win
You know.
Yet here you are
Calling attention
Like it's your best friend.
Because it is.

I see you
Looking
In the mirror.
Don't you.
Don't you.

Remember restaurants? A little food for thought regarding our complex biology.

Restaurant

At tables we sit
Six feet apart
Heat between separates us
Eyes meet
Lingering
It would be
Nice to meet you
Without the company
With the heat
Without the separation
Only the indulgence
Of the menu.

Yes is the answer we all seem to be looking for. Today I looked for it in my backyard.

Backyard

The wind
Blows the same.
The flowers
Bloom like before.
Will we ever
Feel free?
Will we ever be
Uninfected?
Will ever come
Back to yard?
Eventually—the answer is
Yes.

I missed my sister Barbara's birthday. She does not look it, but it was a big one and I miss being able to remember the celebration.

Miss Remembering

Sometimes I miss what never was—
Almost remembering what did not
Happen.

This pandemic schedule has me feeling lazy.

Walls

Can you
Climb walls
while
Sitting in a
Chair?

There's a lot of I in this—sorry. And I'm not this worried, yet.

On Sale

I'm scared
Worried all the time.
I hide it well—sometimes.
I worry about how much
I worry—publicly now.
Worry and I are
Well acquainted,
Even friends
But not real close.
My biggest fear?
Not worrying.
That's terror.
It feels right—scared.
I was made for it.
Perhaps I can capitalize—you know
Sell it.
Would you buy my
Fear?

Sitting on the deck this morning watching my wife enjoy a cup of coffee, I was not lonely.

Q the Day

Is that any way to say
Good morning?
That pose
That smile
That touch
That kiss.
What did I do to
Deserve this?
Am I still
Dreaming?

Acknowledgments

The author is grateful to the editors of the following journals in which poems of this book previously appeared, sometimes in slightly different form or with a different title:

City Lifestyles: "Contender" and "About Why?"

From Whispers to Roars: "On Sale"

Pangolin Review: "Before the Distance II"

The Dewdrop: "Before the Distance"

Virgin Islands Source: "Reputation" and "Cope-Outs"

Special thanks to my friends and family for indulging my many phases and providing endless encouragement of this latest endeavor. Your support and patience mean much more than I can ever put in words. And to my love, Joan, there is no meter without you.

Praise for *Before the Distance*

Before the Distance will take you farther than you thought you had energy to travel in a pandemic . . . to memories you didn't know you had, and through longings you kept secret, even from yourself. It will take you back to the color blue and to the fragrance of lost love. The collection both inhabits and sets free the goblins of uncertainty: free-floating worry, off-kilter encounters, mind games, and coping skills. We can tell Trozzolo is not a young man. He knows shortcuts. With sure-footed prose, he takes us by the hand and shows us to shelter, in places like backyards and morning kisses and winter's end. You will leave his verse infected by questions: "When is my party?," "Does dust make choices?," "What wonder could have flowed?" And eventually, "Did you find your way home?"

—Becky Blades, author
Do Your Laundry or You'll Die Alone

Pasquale Trozzolo's *Before the Distance* is an invitation. Here, we enter the life of a fully lived man in a time of social and global upheaval. But unlike today's social media or news feeds, this is not a rant, and it is not a call for anything. Rather, it's an introspective dialogue between peace and chaos, love and instability, joy and fear. Like a conversation, the poet casually speaks to us, sharing his innermost self as if we're gathered around the table, each truth spoken in the shape of a stanza. They're measured words that carry tenderness and purpose, and they examine the state of our place in the world, the doubts we all carry, the rites of passage we must go through, and the social norms we must now question more than ever in response to COVID. Ultimately, Trozzolo reminds us that we are not in control, and that we are simply navigating our circumstances as best we can. The poet writes,

"Everything seems so big and hard and dangerous/ that we often forget the scale—the one that measures us like a pebble of sand." In this gorgeous debut chapbook, we are reminded to look at our catastrophes and celebrations not as good or bad, but simply, as reality.

—Alan Chazaro, author of *Piñata Theory* and *This Is Not a Frank Ocean Cover Album*

About the Author

Pasquale Trozzolo is an entrepreneur and founder of Trozzolo Communications Group, one of the leading advertising and public relations firms in the Midwest. In addition to building his business he also spent time as a race car driver and grad school professor. Now with too much time on his hands, he continues to complicate his life by living out as many retirement clichés as possible. He's up to the p's. Before the pandemic Trozzolo only shared his poems with a handful of close friends. Since sheltering-at-home he has begun to share what he calls Virus Poems.

<pasqualetrozzolo.com>

About The Poetry Box®

The Poetry Box® is a boutique publishing company that enjoys providing a platform for both established and emerging poets to share their words with the world through beautiful printed books and chapbooks.

Feel free to visit the online bookstore (thePoetryBox.com), where you'll find more titles including:

Epicurean Ecstasy by Cynthia Gallaher

Bee Dance by Cathy Cain

Like the O in Hope by Jeanne Julian

Moroccan Holiday by Lauren Tivey

Shadow Man by Margaret Chula

A Long, Wide Stretch of Calm by Melanie Green

What She Was Wearing by Shawn Aveningo Sanders

The Very Rich Hours by Gregory Loselle

Between States of Matter by Sherry Rind

My Miscellaneous Muse by Ralph La Rosa

Sitting in Powell's Watching Burnside Dissolve in Rain by Doug Stone

*The Kingdom of Bird*s by Joan Colby

and more . . .

www.ingramcontent.com/pod-product-compliance
Lightning Source LLC
LaVergne TN
LVHW020439080526
838202LV00055B/5266